MY FIRST
GREEN
B·O·O·K

ANGELA WILKES

ALFRED A. KNOPF ❧ NEW YORK

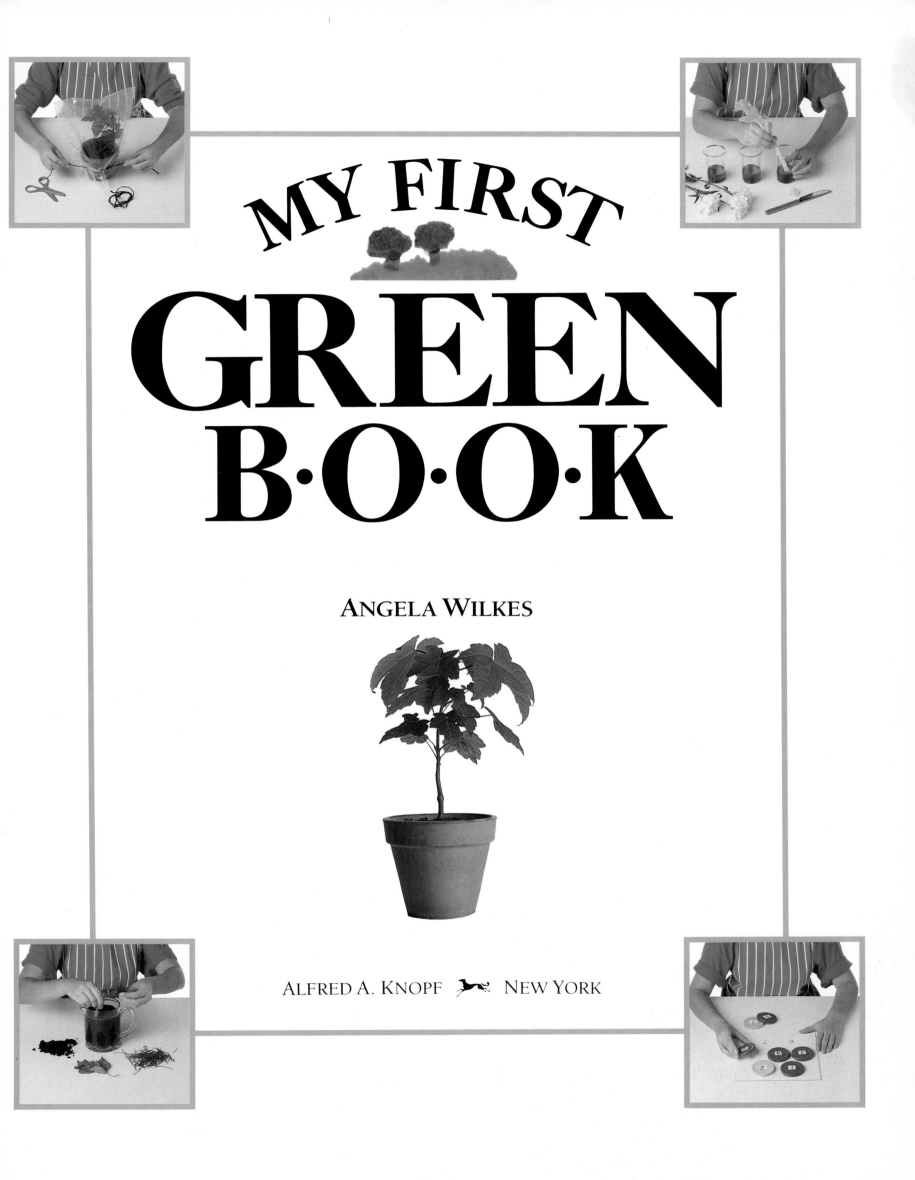

A Dorling Kindersley Book

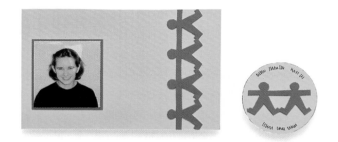

Design Mathewson Bull
Photography Dave King and Mike Dunning
Editor Andrea Pinnington
Production Norina Bremner
Art Director Roger Priddy

This is a Borzoi book published by Alfred A. Knopf, Inc.

First American edition, 1991

2 4 6 8 10 9 7 5 3 1

Library of Congress Cataloging in Publication Data
Wilkes, Angela. My first green book / by Angela Wilkes. p. cm.
Summary: Features environmental activities and projects in such areas as water pollution, recycling, acid rain, and wildlife gardens.

1. Pollution–Juvenile literature. 2. Pollution–Experiments–Juvenile literature. 3. Environmental protection–Juvenile literature. 4. Environmental protection–Experiments–Juvenile literature. 5. Gardening–Juvenile literature. 6. Conservation of natural resources–Juvenile literature.[1. Pollution–Experiments. 2. Environmental protection–Experiments. 3. Conservation of natural resources–Experiments.4. Experiments.] I. Title.

TD176.W55   1991   91-4371   363.7-dc20
ISBN 0-679-81780-8
ISBN 0-679-91780-2 (lib. bdg.)

Phototypeset by Setting Studio, Newcastle
Color reproduction by Colourscan, Singapore
Printed and bound in Italy by L.E.G.O.

Dorling Kindersley would like to thank Jonathan Buckley, Helen Drew, Mandy Earey, Marie Greenwood, Ann Kramer, Steve Parker, and Stephen Webster for their help in producing this book.

Illustrations by Brian Delf

CONTENTS

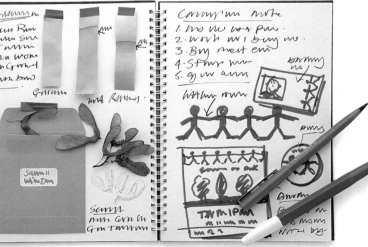

BEING GREEN

Being green is not about changing color. It is about caring for our environment and trying to change the way we do things so that we stop harming and polluting the world around us. Earth is facing massive problems at the moment, but everyone can do something to help. First, though, we have to understand what the problems are; this is what *My First Green Book* sets out to do.

World problems

There are many problems facing our planet. Much of the air is no longer clean to breathe; a lot of the land and many rivers and oceans are polluted. Tropical rain forests are being chopped down. Plants and animals are dying out. And we are using up Earth's supply of fossil fuels, such as oil and coal. *My First Green Book* explains what many of these problems actually mean. It also suggests things that you can do to help solve the problems. Everything that you do, no matter how small, has an effect on the world around you.

Look around you

Being green starts at home. Look at how much the car is used for unnecessary journeys. Look at exactly what your family buys at the stores every week. Once you are aware of what is going on around you, you can try to cut down on waste. That is being green.

Where you live

Once you have started being green at home, you can turn your attention to the town where you live. How clean is the air? Are there any local recycling programs? Start a green diary so that you can make notes of the things you find out.

Action

One of the best ways to help do something about green issues is to join an environmental organization. You can find their addresses at your public library. Or you can set up a campaign group with your friends. Children can help to make the world a better place. The future of Earth is in your hands!

GREEN EXPERIMENTS

My First Green Book is full of fascinating projects and experiments to do at home that will help you understand some of the environmental problems facing our planet. Step-by-step photographs and simple instructions show you exactly what to do, and there are life-size photographs of the materials you need and of the finished projects. On the next page is a list to read before you start. Below are the points to look for in each experiment.

How to use this book

The things you need
The things to collect for each experiment are shown life-size to help you make sure you have everything you need.

Equipment
Illustrated checklists show you the equipment you need to have ready before you start an experiment.

Step-by-step
Step-by-step photographs and clear instructions show you what to do at each stage of the experiment.

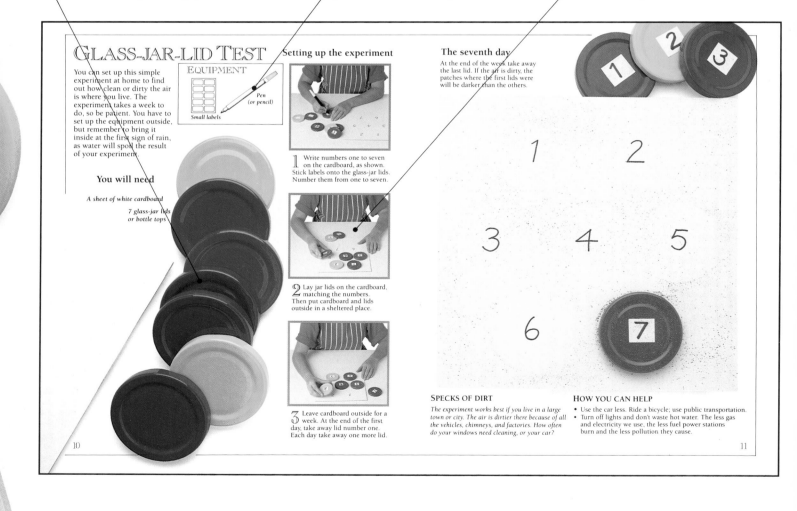

GLASS-JAR-LID TEST

You can set up this simple experiment at home to find out how clean or dirty the air is where you live. The experiment takes a week to do, so be patient. You have to set up the equipment outside, but remember to bring it inside at the first sign of rain, as water will spoil the result of your experiment.

EQUIPMENT

Pen (or pencil)

Small labels

You will need

A sheet of white cardboard

7 glass-jar lids or bottle tops

Setting up the experiment

1 Write numbers one to seven on the cardboard, as shown. Stick labels onto the glass-jar lids. Number them from one to seven.

2 Lay jar lids on the cardboard, matching the numbers. Then put cardboard and lids outside in a sheltered place.

3 Leave cardboard outside for a week. At the end of the first day, take away lid number one. Each day take away one more lid.

The seventh day

At the end of the week take away the last lid. If the air is dirty, the patches where the first lids were will be darker than the others.

SPECKS OF DIRT
The experiment works best if you live in a large town or city. The air is dirtier there because of all the vehicles, chimneys, and factories. How often do your windows need cleaning, or your car?

HOW YOU CAN HELP
• Use the car less. Ride a bicycle; use public transportation.
• Turn off lights and don't waste hot water. The less gas and electricity we use, the less fuel power stations burn and the less pollution they cause.

10

11

Things to remember

1 Read the instructions before you start and gather together everything you need for the experiment.

2 Put on an apron or old shirt and roll up your sleeves. Cover your work table with newspaper.

3 Follow the instructions carefully at each stage of the experiment and do only one thing at a time.

4 Be very careful with sharp scissors. Do not use them unless there is an adult there to help you.

5 Keep a record of each experiment or project and its results in your green diary (see page 44).

6 When you have finished, put everything away, clean up any mess, and wash your hands.

The final results
Life-size photographs show you what happens at the end of the experiment so that you know what to expect.

Explanation
At the end of each experiment you will find a simple explanation of what has happened and why.

How you can help
Many of the experiments are followed by a list of things you can do to help improve environmental problems.

DIRTY-WATER TEST

Have you ever wondered where all your water comes from? The fresh water that pours out of our faucets comes from rivers, lakes, streams, reservoirs, and from deep underground. All living things need water – clean water – but the earth is like a sponge and soaks up anything liquid that is dumped on the ground or into the rivers. This simple experiment shows you what happens when pollutants get into the water system.

EQUIPMENT

3 glass jars

Knife

You will need

A stick of celery

White flowers

Colored ink or food coloring

A pitcher of water

What to do

1 Pour about one inch of food coloring or ink into each glass. Add about one inch of water to each glass.

2 Trim the flower and celery stems. Stand the celery and flowers in colored water and leave them for a few hours.

DIRTY WATER
The plants absorb the colored water. The coloring acts like pollution. As the plants drink the water, they drink up the pollution in it too. The same thing happens to a person or animal that drinks polluted water.

WATER POLLUTION
Factory wastes, pesticides, and fertilizers cause water pollution. But a lot of pollution also starts at home.

HOW YOU CAN HELP
• Encourage your family to use ecologically safe laundry soap and dishwashing liquid.
• Avoid using chemical fertilizers and pesticides in the garden.
• Tell your parents never to pour out chemicals or car oil onto the ground or down the drain.

AIR POLLUTION

Most people assume that the air we breathe is clean, but this is not always so. Factories and power stations pour smoke and poisonous gases into the sky as they produce electricity and goods, and vehicles belch exhaust fumes. All these things *pollute* (make dirty) the air around us. Polluted air is bad for all living things: plants, animals, and people.

You can find out how clean or dirty the air is by looking at trees and at the walls of old stone buildings. Below, you can see some of the signs to look for.

LICHENS

Lichens grow mainly on trees and on the walls of old buildings. As they have no roots or stems, lichens absorb moisture directly from the air or rain, together with any dirt that is in the air. This makes them very sensitive to air pollution. Some lichens grow only in clean air; other, hardier varieties can survive in more polluted air.

LEAFY AND HAIRY LICHENS

Leafy green lichen like this grows on walls and trees. It is a sign that the air is fairly clean. Hairy green "beard lichen" is a sign that the air is very clean.

CRUSTY ORANGE LICHEN

This type of lichen is found on rocks or stones, such as gravestones.

Crusty orange lichen can grow in slightly polluted air.

CRUSTY GREEN LICHENS

Lichens like this grow on trees and rocks. They show that the air is polluted.

POLLUTION IN TOWNS AND CITIES

In a large city no lichens will grow at all, but you can find other signs of air pollution. Many of the buildings look gray or black, but they are not meant to. Find out what they were built from: pale stone, red or yellow brick, for example.

GREEN ALGAE

Powdery green algae such as this can tolerate severe pollution. If there are no lichens, just green algae, the air is probably very dirty.

This broken piece of yellow brick shows the contrast between the brick's original color and its now dirty gray surface.

CLEANING UP THE CITIES

Every year city councils spend a lot of money cleaning buildings and monuments. Here you can see part of Westminster Abbey in London, England, in the process of being cleaned. The stonework on the left has been cleaned; the stonework on the right has not.

If you take a closer look at the dirty stonework, you can see the damage caused by years of air pollution and acid rain (see pages 12-15). Not only have layers of dirt built up, but the harmful chemicals in the air and rain are eating away at the stonework itself.

GLASS-JAR-LID TEST

Setting up the experiment

You can set up this simple experiment at home to find out how clean or dirty the air is where you live. The experiment takes a week to do, so be patient. You have to set up the equipment outside, but remember to bring it inside at the first sign of rain, as water will spoil the result of your experiment.

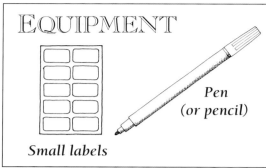

EQUIPMENT

Pen (or pencil)

Small labels

You will need

A sheet of white cardboard

7 glass-jar lids or bottle tops

1 Write numbers one to seven on the cardboard, as shown. Stick labels onto the glass-jar lids. Number them from one to seven.

2 Lay jar lids on the cardboard, matching the numbers. Then put cardboard and lids outside in a sheltered place.

3 Leave cardboard outside for a week. At the end of the first day, take away lid number one. Each day take away one more lid.

The seventh day

At the end of the week take away the last lid. If the air is dirty, the patches where the first lids were will be darker than the others.

1

2

3

4

5

6

7

SPECKS OF DIRT

The experiment works best if you live in a large town or city. The air is dirtier there because of all the vehicles, chimneys, and factories. How often do your windows need cleaning, or your car?

HOW YOU CAN HELP

- Use the car less. Ride a bicycle; use public transportation.
- Turn off lights and don't waste hot water. The less gas and electricity we use, the less fuel power stations burn and the less pollution they cause.

RAIN CHECK

You have probably heard about acid rain, but do you really understand what it is? Here you can find out how to make litmus paper, which scientists use to test substances to see whether or not they are acidic. Then you can try making your own acid water to test. On pages 14 and 15 is a dramatic experiment that shows what acid rain does to plants.

White blotting paper

Vinegar (a weak acid)

You will need

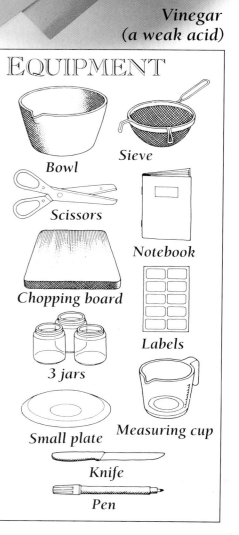

Water

Half a red cabbage

EQUIPMENT

Bowl

Sieve

Scissors

Notebook

Chopping board

Labels

3 jars

Small plate

Measuring cup

Knife

Pen

Making litmus paper

1 Chop up the cabbage* and put it in a bowl. Pour hot water over it and let it soak until the water turns purple.

2 Hold sieve over the measuring cup. Pour cabbage water into the cup through the sieve, so that the cabbage stays in the sieve.

3 Cut some small strips of blotting paper.* Dip them into cabbage water, then lay them on a small plate for a few hours to dry.

12

* Ask an adult to help you with the knife, scissors, and hot water.

The acid test

1 Pour water into one jar and label it. Pour a mixture of three-quarters water and one-quarter vinegar into the second jar.

2 Label the second jar "Slightly acid." Make a mixture of half water and half vinegar in the third jar and label it "Stronger acid."

3 Dip a strip of litmus paper into each jar. What happens to the litmus paper? Write down the results in your notebook.

WHAT HAPPENS

When you dip the litmus paper into plain water, it darkens slightly because it is wet. But when dipped into water with vinegar in it, the litmus paper turns pink, regardless of how much vinegar is in the water.

Strips of litmus paper

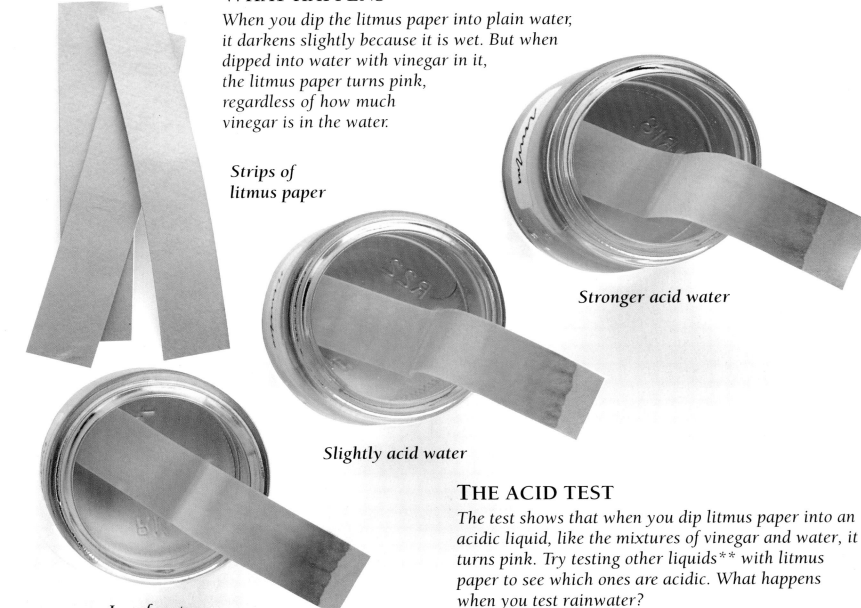

Stronger acid water

Slightly acid water

Jar of water

THE ACID TEST

*The test shows that when you dip litmus paper into an acidic liquid, like the mixtures of vinegar and water, it turns pink. Try testing other liquids** with litmus paper to see which ones are acidic. What happens when you test rainwater?*

** *Check with an adult which liquids are safe to test.*

ACID RAIN

Poisonous gases are constantly being released into the air from factories, power stations, and vehicle exhausts. When some of these gases mix with water, they make the water *acidic*; when these gases mix with rain clouds, they dissolve in the moisture of the clouds and form acid rain. Here you can see how acid rain affects plants.

You will need

Water

Sticky labels

Three green plants* in pots with drip trays

Vinegar

EQUIPMENT

Measuring cup

Pen

3 big glass jars

Plant spray

What to do

1 Fill one of the big jars one-quarter full with vinegar. Fill the remaining three-quarters of the jar with water.

2 Write two labels saying "Slightly acid." Stick one label to the jar of water and vinegar and the other to one of the plant pots.

3 Fill another big jar with water. Write two labels saying "Water." Stick one to the jar and the other to a plant pot.

14

* These should be plants you can allow to die.

ACID RAIN

Acid rain has the same effect on plants as water and vinegar mixed together, but it is weaker and works more slowly. Acid rain is killing forests, poisoning lakes, harming wildlife, and affecting people's health. Everyone can help to stop it.

HOW YOU CAN HELP

- Demand for electricity is the main cause of acid rain, so turn off lights.
- Use cars less.
- Recycle things.

4 Fill the remaining jar with a mixture of half water and half vinegar. Label this and the third plant pot "Stronger acid."

5 Stand the plants in a row. Every day water and spray each one with the mixture from the jar that matches its label.

What happens

The plant that receives clean water remains strong and healthy, but the two other plants soon die. The stronger the acid, the sooner a plant dies.

Healthy green plant

This plant is dying.

This plant has already died.

Water

Slightly acid

Stronger acid

DIRTY-WATER TEST

Have you ever wondered where all your water comes from? The fresh water that pours out of our faucets comes from rivers, lakes, streams, reservoirs, and from deep underground. All living things need water – clean water – but the earth is like a sponge and soaks up anything liquid that is dumped on the ground or into the rivers. This simple experiment shows you what happens when pollutants get into the water system.

EQUIPMENT

3 glass jars

Knife

You will need

A stick of celery

White flowers

Colored ink or food coloring

A pitcher of water

What to do

HOW YOU CAN HELP

- Encourage your family to use ecologically safe laundry soap and dishwashing liquid.
- Avoid using chemical fertilizers and pesticides in the garden.
- Tell your parents never to pour chemicals or car oil onto the ground or down the drain.

1 Pour about one inch of food coloring or ink into each glass. Add about one inch of water to each glass.

2 Trim the flower and celery stems.* Stand the celery and flowers in colored water and leave them for a few hours.

DIRTY WATER

The plants absorb the colored water. The coloring acts like pollution. As the plants drink the water, they drink up the pollution in it too. The same thing happens to a person or animal that drinks polluted water.*

WATER POLLUTION

Factory wastes, pesticides, and fertilizers cause water pollution. But a lot of pollution also starts at home.

* Ask an adult to help you.

CLEANING WATER

We expect clean drinking water whenever we turn on the faucet. But because most of our water comes from rivers, reservoirs, and under the ground, it often starts off dirty. It has run through rocks and soil, and it contains the wastes of animals and plants and polluting chemicals. To make it safe to drink, the water we use in our homes has to be specially cleaned at a water purification plant before it reaches our faucets. Try constructing this water filter to find out how it is done.

A pitcher of water

Soil

EQUIPMENT

2 pitchers

Pen

A large spoon

Scissors

You will need

Grass and leaves

Blotting paper

Gravel or small pebbles

Coarse sand

A clean flowerpot

18

Making the water filter

1 Spoon some small amounts of soil, sand, gravel, grass, and leaves into the pitcher of water. Stir everything together.

2 Stand the flowerpot on the blotting paper and draw around the base of the pot. Cut the circle out of the blotting paper.*

3 Put the circle of blotting paper at the bottom of the flowerpot. Fill the pot halfway with sand, then add a layer of gravel.

*Ask an adult to help you.

Using the water filter

Stand the flowerpot filter on top of the empty pitcher. Slowly pour the muddy water into the filter.

What happens

The water that runs out of the filter is cleaner than the water poured in because the filter traps a lot of dirt. The filters at a purification plant are very thick and make water much cleaner. Then special chemicals are added to the water to kill any germs.

Muddy water

Flowerpot filter

The water runs out through the hole in the bottom of the flowerpot filter

Cleaner, filtered water

DO NOT DRINK FILTERED WATER

19

ROTTING AWAY

Why isn't the earth covered with organic waste: dead leaves, the bodies of animals, and old trees? The red-pepper test below will help you to understand how nature gets rid of and recycles its waste.

Do you ever wonder what happens to people's garbage? Most of it is buried and cannot be recycled. Do the test at the bottom of the page to find out what happens to some garbage.

The red-pepper test

You can do this test with a red pepper, or with other foods, such as a piece of bread, a small piece of cheese, or an apple core.

Slice the red pepper in half (so that you can see inside it).* Put half the pepper (or any other piece of food you are using) in a plastic bag and tie the top of the bag firmly. Then just leave it for a week or two.

Look at the food every day and make notes of what happens to it in your green diary (see page 44). Do not open the plastic bag and touch the food. The red pepper was photographed without its bag to make it easier to see.

Day 1   *Day 5*

The burial test

To find out what things rot, try burying the objects on the right in separate holes in the garden. Mark where the holes are, then dig the objects up a month later. Which are rotting? Turn the page to find out about recycling garbage that does not biodegrade.

A leafy twig

A plastic-foam egg carton

An empty can

* *Ask an adult to help you.*

NATURE'S RECYCLERS

As the days go by, the red pepper shrivels up and gets moldy. After two weeks it has shrunk. What happens is that the mold actually eats the pepper. Molds are a type of fungus. They are in the air all around you, but they are so tiny that they are invisible. Molds land on food and eat it. Other fungi, bacteria, worms, mites, insects, and other creatures do the same with dead plants and animals. They clear away nature's waste by breaking it down into minerals and humus (pages 28-29) in the soil, which can then be used as food by newly growing plants and animals. Things that rot like this are said to be "biodegradable."

Day 8   Day 10   Day 15

Pieces of paper and newspaper   A piece of cotton or wool fabric   An empty bottle   An apple core

21

Your Garbage

Every year the average household throws away a huge amount of trash – probably at least 300-500 garbage bags full. Most of it ends up in garbage dumps or buried in pits. Either way, the enormous amount of garbage and the nasty mixture of things that go into it are causing a huge pollution problem.

Luckily you can do a lot to help solve the problem. Most of our garbage can be reused or *recycled*. This means that fewer new things have to be made, which saves energy and reduces pollution. Try sorting your garbage into the groups below. At the bottom of the page you can find out what to do with them.

METALS

Magnet

Most food cans and some bottle and soda-can tops are made of steel. These stick to a magnet.

Aluminum does not stick to a magnet.

Sort steel and aluminum cans from your garbage and take them to the nearest recycling center. These centers are often near big supermarkets. Other things made of aluminum, such as aluminum foil, pie plates, and frozen-food trays, can also be recycled.

GLASS

Perfume bottles

Glass jar

Bottles

If bottles are returnable, return them to where you bought them so they can be reused. All other glass bottles and jars can be taken to a recycling center. Remove all bottle tops and lids and sort the glass by color, into the brown, green, and clear containers.

PAPER

Used envelopes and writing paper

Magazines, news-papers

Cardboard

Paper is made from trees. Making new paper uses up millions of trees each year. You can help by taking your newspapers and other wastepaper to the local recycling center. You can also reuse paper at home by writing on both sides.

ORGANIC WASTE

Dead leaves

Fruit pit

Vegetable trimmings

Dead flowers

Potato peelings

Onion skins

Eggshells

Grass cuttings

Flower petals

About one-third of your trash is made up of organic waste – things that are biodegradable and rot naturally. If you have a garden, persuade your parents to make a compost pile. All organic waste can go onto it, and it will rot down to make fertile soil.

RUMMAGE SALE

Old clothes

Old toys in good condition

Old baby clothes

Old books

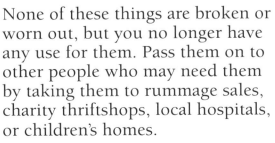

Leftover fabric and yarn

None of these things are broken or worn out, but you no longer have any use for them. Pass them on to other people who may need them by taking them to rummage sales, charity thriftshops, local hospitals, or children's homes.

PLASTICS AND MIXED MATERIALS

Plastic bottles, bags, and wrapping

Plastic packaging

Plastics are almost indestructible. Some plastics, like soda bottles, can be recycled. But the best way to avoid having to throw them away is to not buy them in the first place.

PACKAGING

One of the main sources of everyday waste is packaging. Packaging can be useful. It protects goods and may provide useful information about them. But many things come in layers and layers of unnecessary paper, plastic, and cardboard. Usually the more expensive a product is, the more layers of wasteful packaging it has.

The best way to reduce waste is to avoid buying anything that is overpackaged. Here you can see the amount of packaging used for a take-out meal for one child.

The food

Tomato ketchup

Small portion of French fries

Small hamburger

Drink

Fruit tart

The packaging

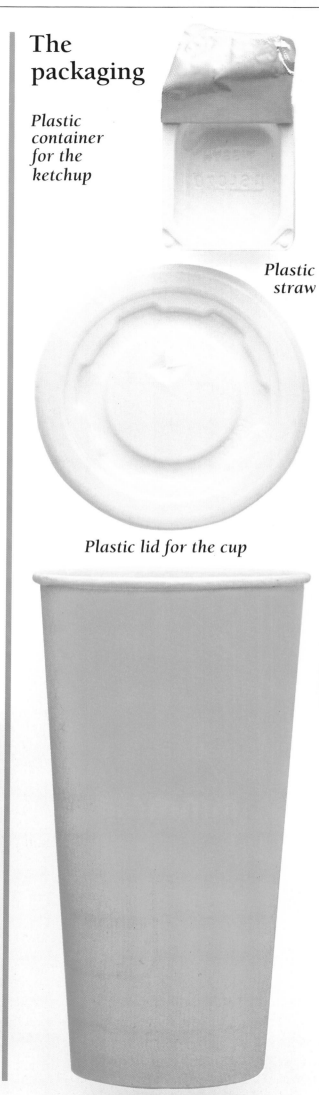

Plastic container for the ketchup

Plastic straw

Plastic lid for the cup

Cardboard cup

Paper napkin

Cardboard container for the French fries

Cardboard container for the fruit tart

Plastic-foam container for the hamburger

AVOIDING WASTE

All the packaging here will go straight into the wastebasket. To avoid such waste, try the following:

- Complain about unnecessary packaging in restaurants.
- If something is overpackaged, do not buy it.
- Avoid buying small, individually wrapped items.
- Take your own bags with you when you go shopping so you do not need the endless bags that stores give out.

Paper bag to put everything in

Green Shopping

When you go shopping for food and household goods, you are faced with a huge choice of things to buy. Some of them are "greener" than others – they are better for you and less harmful to our planet. The more green products you buy, the more stores have to stock them and the cheaper they will become. Below are some guidelines on what to look for when shopping.

Whole foods

Refined white rice

Natural brown rice

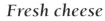

Fresh cheese

Processed cheese

Processed food may be colored, bleached, refined, specially packaged, or have had chemicals added. Read the labels on packages and try to avoid processed food.

Fresh is best

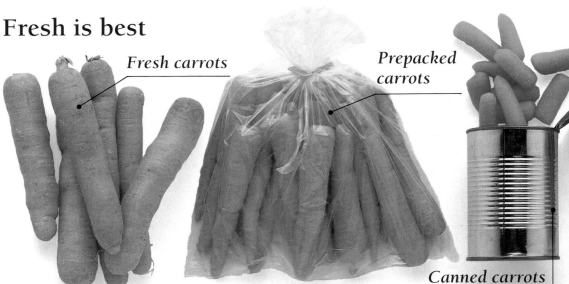

Fresh carrots

Prepacked carrots

Canned carrots

When faced with a choice like this, go for the fresh food with the least packaging. You do not need plastic bags around everything. Canned food, although cheap, may not be as good for you as fresh food, and its manufacture wastes both metal and fuel.

Organic produce

Organic apples

Non-organic apples, wrapped in plastic

Organic fruit and vegetables are produced on farms that do not use chemical fertilizers or pesticides. Organic food costs more than food grown with chemicals, but the more of it that people buy, the cheaper and more widely available it will become.

Eggs

Free-range eggs

Factory farm eggs

Most hens that lay our eggs spend their entire lives in cramped wire cages. If you want to discourage this type of egg production, choose *free-range* eggs. These are laid by hens that are given space to wander. Avoid buying eggs in plastic-foam cartons.

Recycled paper

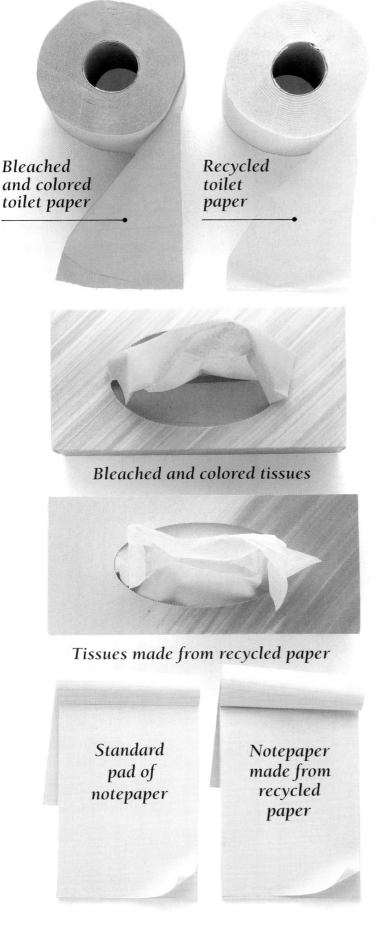

Bleached and colored toilet paper

Recycled toilet paper

Bleached and colored tissues

Tissues made from recycled paper

Standard pad of notepaper

Notepaper made from recycled paper

In most supermarkets you can now buy products made from recycled paper. They look like the things made from new paper, but no trees have been cut down to make them.

Aerosols

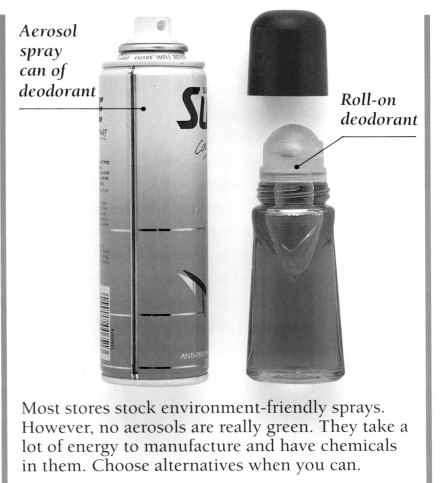

Aerosol spray can of deodorant

Roll-on deodorant

Most stores stock environment-friendly sprays. However, no aerosols are really green. They take a lot of energy to manufacture and have chemicals in them. Choose alternatives when you can.

Cleaning materials

Standard household liquid soap

Environment-friendly household liquid soap

You can now buy liquid soaps, laundry powders, and other cleaning materials that are free of harmful chemicals and strong detergents. Buying these helps to reduce water pollution.

SOIL TEST

Do you know what soil is? It is not just dirt, but a mixture of all kinds of things. The basis of soil is finely ground-up rocks and minerals from the earth's surface. Plants, worms, insects, and other creatures live on this ground-up rock, then die and rot. Their remains form organic matter called *humus*, which rots down into minerals. To find out more about soil, collect as many different types as you can and do this test on them.

Different types of soil

Garden soil

You will need

A big pitcher of water

Farmland soil

Woodland soil

EQUIPMENT

Three glass jars

Big spoon

Pen

Labels

What to do

1 Spoon a different type of soil into each jar until it is about a third full. Label the lid of each jar with the type of soil in it.

2 Fill the jars with water and put the lids on. Shake the jars to mix the soil and water, then let them settle for a few days.

GARDEN SOIL

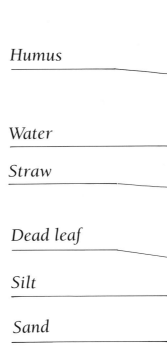

Humus

Water

Humus

Clay

Silt

This soil was collected from a city garden. It contains a lot of silt and clay, but not much humus.

FARMLAND SOIL

Humus

Water

Straw

Dead leaf

Silt

Sand

Farmland soil varies depending on the area it is in, what is being farmed, and whether the farmer farms organically.

WOODLAND SOIL

Humus (leaf litter)

Water

Clay and silt

This soil was collected from an oak forest and contains a lot of leaf litter from the autumn leaves.

DIFFERENT LAYERS

After a few days the soil in each jar settles into different layers. The heavier parts settle first and the lightest ones – the humus – last. Look at these pictures and ask an adult to help you identify what each type of soil is made of. Then compare the soils. Which type contains the most humus? Which type do you think plants will grow in the best? Compare soil from sand dunes or a bag of compost from a garden center.

WHY SOIL IS IMPORTANT

Each type of soil is made up of different amounts of gravel, sand, silt, clay, and humus, and different plants grow on each one. You would not expect to find the same plants growing on a sand dune and in a forest or woodland, for example. Humus acts like a natural fertilizer; it also holds soil together so that it cannot be blown or washed away easily. Without soil, most plants could not grow. Organic gardening and farming methods take the best care of the soil by constantly replacing its organic matter.

MAKING A WILDLIFE GARDEN

One of the best ways to help wildlife flourish close to your home is to create a special garden. You don't need much space. A window box or a large pot will do. Plant the garden with nectar-rich flowers and it will attract butterflies and bees. Here you can see how to plant a window box with late summer flowers.*

EQUIPMENT

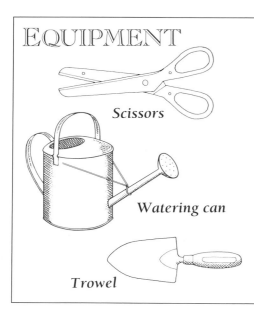

Scissors

Watering can

Trowel

A window box or large flowerpot with drainage holes in the bottom

You will need

Heather

Gravel or clay pellets

Soil-based potting compost

What to do

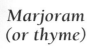
*Marjoram
(or thyme)*

1 Fill the bottom of the window box with a layer of gravel or pellets about 1 inch deep. This lets excess water drain from the soil.

2 With the trowel put potting compost into the window box, on top of the gravel. The window box needs to be half full.

*Showy
sedum*

3 Keeping the plants in their pots, decide how to arrange them. Tall plants should go at the back and trailing ones at the front.

4 Gently take the first plant out of its pot and put it in the window box. Press it slightly into the compost.

*Chrysanthemums
and asters*

5 Do the same with the other plants. Fill potting compost in around the plants. Press it down firmly, then water it well.

For suggestions on other plants, turn to page 34.

31

WILDLIFE GARDEN

And here is the finished window box, full of flowers that will last through late summer. Put the window box on a sunny window ledge, making sure that it is stable and cannot fall. Even if you live in the heart of a city, you will be able to watch the bees and butterflies come in search of nectar. Turn the page for more ideas on plants to attract wildlife.

DAISY HEADS

Most daisy-like flowers are popular with butterflies and bees. In late summer these creatures flock to daisy-type chrysanthemums, asters, and sunflowers.

SWEET MARJORAM

The pink flowers of this strongly scented herb attract both bees and butterflies. Another herb that you could use is thyme, which also has small, pretty flowers.

Watering

Water the window box often enough to keep the compost moist. It will need watering every day during warm weather.

SHOWY SEDUM

A garden plant famous for attracting butterflies, the showy sedum has wide heads of tightly packed tiny pink flowers in late summer. It flowers year after year.

HEATHER

This small evergreen shrub produces spikes of pink or purple bell-shaped flowers from midsummer to late fall. It is very popular with bees.

WINDOW BOX

This window box is made of terra cotta, or clay, rather than plastic. Terra cotta absorbs a lot of moisture, so terra-cotta window boxes and flowerpots need watering more often than plastic ones.

Deadheading

The plants in the window box will flower longer if you regularly pick or snip off dead flower heads.*

* Ask an adult to help you.

PLANTS FOR THE BIRDS AND BEES

If you have a garden at home or school, there are many plants that you can grow to attract wildlife. Make sure there are plenty of spring flowers, such as aubrietia, wallflowers, and honesty, to provide nectar for the butterflies early in the year. A patch of stinging nettles will supply food for the caterpillars of many butterflies. Below are some good plants to grow for the birds and the bees.

HAWTHORN

Hawthorn is a wonderful shrub for wildlife. The flowers are rich in nectar for insects, and the berries attract birds in autumn.

LAVENDER

Lavender, a traditional garden plant, has strongly scented flowers that butterflies love.

LACE-CAP HYDRANGEA

Lace-cap hydrangeas flower late in the summer. They have lots of tiny flowers that attract honeybees.

Buddleia

Sunflow

Sweet scabious

BLACKBERRIES

Blackberry blossoms
attract bees and
butterflies, and birds
flock to eat the
blackberries, which
fruit in autumn.

GIANT SEED HEADS

Giant sunflowers are great
fun to grow, and in fall the
huge, shaggy seed heads are
a treasure trove for birds. They
perch and sway on the dead
flower heads while pecking
out the oily seeds.

PYRACANTHA

Early in autumn this
striking garden shrub
is laden with bright
berries that birds
like to eat.

BUDDLEIA

Often called the
butterfly bush, buddleia
has scented flowers that attract
both bees and
butterflies.

SEA HOLLY

This is one of a family of bee plants.
The thistle-like flowers appear in
late summer.

Sunflower seeds

SUNFLOWER

In late summer butterflies, bees, and some
small beetles are attracted to the open-faced
blooms of sunflowers and other
daisy-like flowers.

SWEET SCABIOUS

Sweet scabious attracts bees and other insects.
It is a sweetly scented annual (a plant that
lives for one year) and flowers in late summer.

PLANTING A TREE

Trees are precious. Every mature tree provides food and a home for all sorts of birds, insects, and other animals. Yet every day thousands of trees are cut down to make wood for construction, to make paper,* or to clear land for farming. We need to plant more trees – especially broad-leaved trees, which make good homes for wildlife. Here you can learn how to plant trees of your own. On pages 38 to 41 you can find out more about why trees are vital to the health of our planet.

You will need

Different types of tree seed that you can find locally. You will need to collect these in fall.

Maple seeds

Beechnuts

Acorns from oak tree

Horse chestnuts

Seed compost

Sweet chestnuts

Gravel

EQUIPMENT

Plant labels

Watering can

Flowerpots

Trowel

Pen

What to do

1 Put about 0.5 in of gravel into base of each flowerpot. Fill the rest of each pot to just below the top with seed compost.

2 Plant a different tree seed in each flowerpot. Push the seeds about 0.5 in down into the seed compost. Water the compost.

3 Label each flowerpot with the name of the tree. Then put the flowerpots outside and wait until spring to see which seeds grow.

Fast-growing evergreens are planted specially for paper.

THE GROWING TREE

Water the flowerpots regularly to keep the compost moist. By spring some of the tree seeds will have started to grow. Keep a record of the trees' progress in your green diary (see page 44). Measure how fast they grow and note when they grow new leaves.

THE GROWING SEEDLING

This young maple tree is nearing the end of its second summer. As the tree grows, its stem becomes stronger and more woody, like a tiny trunk.

MOVING ON

Baby trees should be planted outside once they are 4 to 5 inches tall. Dig a hole in the ground a little bigger than the pot. Take the tree and compost out of the pot and plant them in the hole.

WHERE TO PLANT?

Ask an adult where it is safe to plant your tree. It should be in a sunny but sheltered spot away from roads or buildings. Continue to care for it once it has been planted outside.

37

TREE TEST

Trees and other green plants play an important part in helping to keep the air around us clean and healthy to breathe. You have already seen how plants take in water (pages 16-17). Try this experiment with a tree seedling, which shows what happens to some of the water that trees drink. It also shows the fascinating effects that trees have on the climate. Then turn the page to read about tropical rain forests and what is happening to them.

(pages 16-17) ... Then turn the page to read about tropical rain forests and what is happening to them.

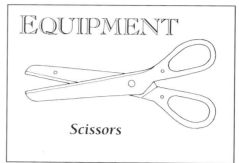

EQUIPMENT

Scissors

A large, clear, plastic bag

You will need

String

A tree seedling (or green plant)

What to do

1 Check that the tree seedling has been watered. Then carefully pull the plastic bag down over the tree, as shown.

2 Tie the plastic bag in place with a piece of string. Stand the plant on a sunny windowsill for a few days.

TREE IN A WET BAG

Look at the plastic bag every day and you will soon notice drops of water collecting on the inside of it. On warm days a lot of water will appear. The tree has tiny holes called stomata in its leaves. Tiny droplets of water evaporate through these holes all the time, but they are so small that you cannot see them. On a hot day a big tree can lose thousands of quarts of water through its leaves in this way.

BUSY LEAVES

A tree's leaves are like busy science laboratories. The tiny holes in the leaves are not just used to "sweat" out water. The tree also breathes through them.

The leaves absorb light from the sun and a gas called carbon dioxide from the air. They combine these with water to make the sugars that the tree needs in order to feed and grow.

At the same time the leaves of the tree give off a gas called oxygen. This is very useful, as it is the gas that humans and all other animals and plants need to breathe.

SAVE TREES!

Too much carbon dioxide pollutes the air, so by absorbing carbon dioxide, trees play a vital role in keeping the air fresh. Vehicles, factories, and power stations produce massive amounts of carbon dioxide by burning fuels such as coal and oil. But there are no longer enough trees to absorb all the carbon dioxide. We must all try to save trees.

HOW YOU CAN HELP

- Plant and care for trees.
- Recycle all the paper you use.
- Save energy (see page 11).

TREASURES OF THE RAIN FOREST

Rain forests are dense, steamy forests that grow in the tropics, where it is very hot and rains almost every day. The trees reach enormous heights and provide a home for many people and the greatest variety of plant and animal life in the world. There are so many trees that they even affect the weather.

Yet people are cutting the trees down – for timber, to clear land for farming, and for roads, houses, and industries. Losing the rain forests means that millions of types of plants and animals will vanish forever. Thousands of people are losing their homes, and world weather may be changing. Here you can read about some of the things that come from the rain forests.

Two types of mahogany

One of the world's largest butterflies, the rare Queen Alexandra's bird wing

PRECIOUS TREES

Many trees such as mahogany, teak, and ebony are cut down because their wood is highly valued. Help save the rain forests by persuading your family not to buy anything made of these woods.

ENDANGERED CREATURES

The loss of animals' homes and food means that many creatures have now become extinct or, like the butterfly above, are in danger of extinction.

RARE PLANTS

Rain forest plants could be a vital source of new foods and raw materials for new medicines. As the forests are destroyed, thousands of species of plants are dying out completely.

Tropical moth orchid

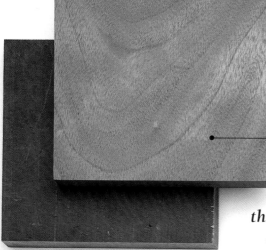

MEDICINES

Thousands of rain forest plants contain things that can be used in medicines. In fact, one in four medicines contains substances derived from rain forest plants.

Medicine

Cardamoms

Cloves

Cinnamon

Nutmegs

RUBBER

Most of the world's natural rubber is made from white latex, which is tapped from the bark of trees that originally came from the Amazon rain forest.

SPICES

Many of the spices used in cooking are produced from trees that come from tropical forests. They include ginger, cloves, cinnamon, mace, nutmeg, allspice, and cardamom.

Cashew nuts

Brazil nuts

Pineapple

NUTS

Brazil nuts come from the Amazon rain forest. The trees on which they grow have never been successfully grown in plantations, so all Brazil nuts have to be gathered from wild trees.

CROPS

Half of the world's main crops were originally discovered in the tropical forests. These include oranges, lemons, pineapples, coffee, rice, corn, sugar, and bananas.

Vegetable oil

OILS

Many rain forest plants are rich in oils. People in the tropics use them in the same way that we use olive oil and diesel oil.

Orange

Lemon

CAMPAIGNER'S KIT

One of the best ways to help make the world a better place is to campaign to improve things. This means spreading information about what is wrong, and suggesting practical ideas on what to do about it. First, collect some of the things shown below to make a campaigner's kit. On pages 44 and 45 you can find out how to collect useful information in a special green book; pages 46 and 47 will show you how to set up your own campaign.

You will need

A notebook, for jotting down information

A small camera, for taking photos when conducting surveys

A pencil

Writing paper and plenty of envelopes, so that you can write letters to people who may be able to help you

An envelope file, for storing copies of your letters and useful newspaper clippings

Colored felt pens

Thumbtacks, for pinning up campaign posters and other information (see pages 46-47)

Large pieces of colored paper and tissue paper, to make into posters

Poster paints and a paintbrush. You need these and the felt pens for making posters for your campaigns.

Scissors

Glue stick

Paper bags, for collecting samples

Sticky labels, for labeling samples that you find

Cardboard and small safety pins, to make into badges

Cellophane tape (for badges)

YOUR GREEN DIARY

To become really aware of what is going on around you, keep a green diary. In your diary you can make notes of what is happening in your town, keep records of your green experiments, and jot down the results of any surveys you make. You can also stick in news clippings and seeds you find for your wildlife garden. Your green diary will be a valuable source of information if you want to set up a campaign (see pages 46-47).

NEWS CLIPPINGS

Ask an adult to help you cut "green issue" articles from newspapers and magazines; stick them in your diary.

(see pages 46-47)

GREEN EXPERIMENTS
Make notes of exactly what happens when you do green experiments. Draw the results, or tape them into the diary, if you can.

Rain check   a)   b)

Made litmus paper from blotting paper. Used it to check
a) Water
b) Water and a little vinegar
c) Water and a lot of vinegar

Water

Slightly acid   Strong

Tree

Samm 11 WhmDm

Maple seeds found near Sam's house: 9-28-91

notes

Lilium tigri... ...m spl... dens. Lilium specio... rubru... crims...

POLLUTION CHECK

Whether you are at home, at school, out visiting, or on vacation, look for evidence of air pollution (see pages 8-9). Make notes and, if you can, drawings of what you find.

Air pollution

Have found two more samples for my pollution check: a piece of bark from Richmond Park and a rock from a beach in Sunset.

Green club

Ideas for things to make for our Green club.

membership card

Poster

Badge

CAMPAIGNING

If you are planning to start a green club or set up a campaign, use your green diary to make notes of your campaign points and to draw ideas for posters, badges, and membership cards.

45

CAMPAIGNING

The best way to improve things in the area where you live is to set up a green campaign group with friends or at school. You might want to start a litter-collecting campaign, set up a recycling program, or create a wildlife garden. Below are some useful things for your campaign group to make.

Logo (club symbol) of row of little green people holding hands, made of folded paper.

LAKEWOOD GREEN CLUB

SAVE OUR PARK

Trees made out of torn-up pieces of tissue paper glued onto the paper poster.

POSTERS

Make posters to pin up locally so that people know what your group is campaigning for. If you are going to hold a meeting, say what the meeting is about and when and where it will be held.

Come to a meeting at Lakewood School at 5 p.m. on March 26th, 1992

46

Making badges

1 For each badge you want to make, draw a small circle on a piece of cardboard. Use a small lid or a glass to draw around.

2 Draw a picture on each badge. Write a slogan around the picture, such as PLANT MORE TREES. Cut out the badges.*

3 Open some small safety pins. Tape the back of each safety pin to a badge,* then carefully close the safety pins again.

MEMBERSHIP CARD

LAKEWOOD GREEN CLUB
MEMBERSHIP CARD

Mandy Smith
5 Rose Avenue
Lakewood

Make a membership card for each member of the group. Glue a small photo of the member to the card and write in his or her name and the name of the group.

BADGES

Save-the-wildlife badge

Stop pollution badge

Club logo badge

Save-the-trees badge

Make a badge with the group logo on it for everyone in the group. Draw a picture on each badge and label it with the name of the group and its campaign.

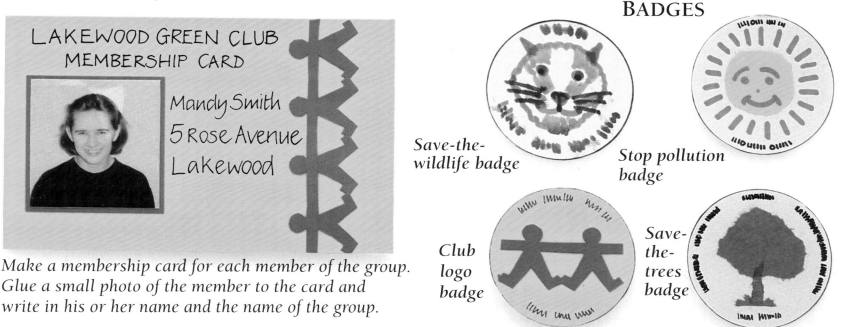

5 Rose Avenue,
Lakewood
March 6th, 1992

Dear Sir,
I am writing to protest the planned closing of Mitchell Park. I

WRITING LETTERS

Write letters to the local paper, to your senator and representative, and to the President about things that you think are wrong. Write your address in the top right corner of the letter, with the date beneath it. Sign and print your name at the end of the letter.

47

*Ask an adult to help you.

GREEN CODE

Find out as much as you can about
environmental problems. Get your family
and friends interested too.

Do not use the car unless you have to.
Walk, bicycle, or use public transportation.

Recycle your garbage (see pages 22-23).

Take care of your pets and plants.

Never litter. Pick up litter you see
lying on the ground.

Do not waste electricity or water.
Remember to turn off lights and faucets.

Look carefully at what you buy (see pages
26-27). Avoid buying overpackaged goods,
processed foods, strong chemicals, and
other wasteful or harmful items.

Avoid using chemical pesticides
or fertilizers in your garden.

Begin a campaign to stop pollution or to save
an area of unused land for wildlife.